JOHN PAUL II

JOHN PAUL II

A Saint for Canada

FR. THOMAS ROSICA, CSB

NOVALIS

© 2014 Novalis Publishing Inc.

Cover design and layout: Audrey Wells
Cover photograph: © Concacan Inc., 1984. All rights reserved. Used with permission.
Interior photographs: Pages 13, 19, 39, 49, 61, 71, 79, 89: From the World Youth Day
2002 Photo archives housed at the Salt and Light Catholic Media Foundation.
Page 25: © Concacan Inc., 1984. All rights reserved. Used with permission.
Page 35: Stanislaw Stolarczyk/FAKTY

Published by Novalis

Publishing Office
10 Lower Spadina Avenue, Suite 400
Toronto, Ontario, Canada
M5V 2Z2

Head Office
4475 Frontenac Street
Montréal, Québec, Canada
H2H 2S2

www.novalis.ca

Library and Archives Canada Cataloguing in Publication

Rosica, Thomas, author   John Paul II : a saint for Canada / Fr. Thomas Rosica.
ISBN 978-2-89646-638-2 (pbk.)

   1. John Paul II, Pope, 1920-2005.   2. Papal visits--Canada.
3. Popes--Biography.   I. Title.

BX1378.5.R68 2014   282.092   C2014-900792-2

Printed in Canada.

We acknowledge the financial support of the Government of Canada through the
Canada Book Fund for business development activities.

5   4   3   2   1   18   17   16   15   14

TABLE OF CONTENTS

INTRODUCTION:
"SANTO SUBITO!"

When the throngs of people began chanting *"Santo subito!"* at the end of Pope John Paul II's funeral mass on April 8, 2005, what were they really saying? They were crying out that in Karol Wojtyla, they saw someone who lived with God and lived with us. He was a sinner who experienced God's mercy and forgiveness. He was the prophetic teacher who preached the Word in season and out of season. He looked at us, loved us, touched us, healed us and gave us hope. He taught us not to be afraid. He showed us how to live, how to love, how to forgive and how to die. He taught us how to embrace the cross in the most excruciating moments of life, knowing that the cross was not God's final answer.

He belonged to the entire world, but in a special way, he belonged to Canadians. More than any other pope in history, John Paul II had made his mark in this country, blessing and speaking to people from coast to coast. He even made a special trip back to a distant Aboriginal community in the far north just to keep a promise. He brought the papacy home to us, shared his concerns – and listened to ours – and made us believe he had seen into our souls. This book is about that special relationship.

That a person is declared "Blessed" or "Saint" is not a statement about perfection. It does not mean that the person was without imperfection, blindness, deafness or sin. Nor is it a 360-degree evaluation of the pontificate or of the Vatican. Beatification and canonization mean that a person lived his or her life with God, relying totally on God's infinite mercy, going forward with God's strength and power, believing in the impossible, loving enemies and persecutors, forgiving in the midst of evil and violence, hoping beyond all hope, and leaving the world a better place. That person lets those around him or her know that there is a force or spirit animating his or her life that is not of this world, but of the next. Such a person lets us catch a glimpse of the greatness and holiness to which we are all called, and shows us the face of God as we journey on our pilgrim way on earth.

In the life of Karol Wojtyla, the boy from Wadowice, Poland, who would grow up to be a priest and Bishop of Krakow, the Bishop of Rome, and a hero for the ages, holiness was contagious. We have all been touched and changed by it. Pope John Paul II was not only "Holy Father" but "a Father who was and is holy." At his funeral mass, Cardinal Joseph Ratzinger (soon to become Pope Benedict XVI) told the world that the Holy Father was watching us and blessing us "from the window of the Father's House." What a declaration of holiness and proximity to God!

Canadians had this taste of holiness firsthand in three visits during John Paul II's pontificate. The September 1984 cross-Canada tour is still within living memory for many thousands of people – and not just Catholics – who thronged to the stadiums, the roadsides and the made-to-order worship sites to listen to this charismatic holy man. At that time, he was still handsome, hale and strong – a captivating presence on stage or in person. Whether he was blessing the fishing fleet in Flatrock, Newfoundland, or meeting with Polish families in Toronto or the sick and elderly at the Martyrs' Shrine near Midland, Ontario, he enthralled us. His love-filled gaze took us in, and we returned the favour.

Bad weather forced the cancellation of a visit prepared for Fort Simpson, Northwest Territories, where John Paul II was to meet with First Nations peoples. The pope felt so deeply sad about missing this visit with them that he promised to return. And he did, in 1987, when he spoke to Aboriginal peoples gathered from across the North. His reverence for the First Nations peoples and compassion for their history of suffering helped change the way Canadians viewed their own troubled relationship with their Aboriginal sisters and brothers.

To some, those visits from the 1980s might seem like past history. For Canadians under the age of 30, when you mention this pope's name, they remember one event: World Youth Day 2002 in Toronto. This momentous occasion, one of a long line of World Youth Days that began early in this pontificate, drew hundreds of thousands of young Catholics – and some not-so-young along with some not-so-Catholic – to get a glimpse of the pope over a week-long festival of worship, prayer, spiritual formation and camaraderie. For that week, the youth of the world turned Toronto into a city-wide festival; subway cars, streetcars, buses and the streets themselves rang with laughter and singing (yes, singing!) as these young Catholics burned with faith.

That week, Pope John Paul II told the young of the world – as he had done so many times before – "Do not be afraid" to live out your faith and be the best you can be. The pope went home after an exhausting outdoor Mass with more than 850,000 people at Toronto's Downsview Park. The young went home with joy in their hearts to live what they had seen and felt during that privileged week. The event had ripple effects across the country, as many of the young, particularly the thousands of volunteers, continued to network with each other and share their gifts with the Church, either as young professionals in communications and ministry, or as volunteers in their parishes and schools. Even today, those participants at WYD 2002, now more than a decade older, recall this period with great fondness. Many trace their conversion to Catholicism to that luminous summer week in Toronto.

This book before you is not a history of the pope's trips to Canada, nor a scholarly analysis of his impact on the Church here or even of Catholicism in general. Rather, it is a spiritual reflection based on my own personal involvement with this amazing holy man and my experience at the heart of World Youth Day 2002 and since. If it has an emphasis on the young, it is because the youth had a special place in this pope's heart, demonstrated in so much of what he said and did. Today, many younger Catholics call themselves "John Paul II Catholics," meaning that they came of age during this papacy and that their own understanding of being Catholic in the world today is marked by this one man.

These pages contain recollections of what it was like to be engaged in the Church during those tumultuous events in Canada, but more than that, the book explores what Pope John Paul's messages mean for us: for who we are as Catholics and human beings, and for how we live our lives and relate to each other. It is, in effect, a testimony to his impact on this country.

Three years ago, in 2011, we celebrated the beatification of Pope John Paul II. On April 27, 2014, he is being enrolled in the book of Saints of the Catholic Church. May we learn from "Papa Wojtyla" how to cross thresholds, open doors, build bridges, embrace the cross of suffering and proclaim the Gospel of Life to the people of our time. May we learn how to live, to suffer and to die unto the Lord. Let us pray that we may receive a small portion of the fidelity of Peter's witness and the boldness of Paul's proclamation that were so mightily present in Karol Wojtyla – Saint John Paul II. May he intercede for us and for all those who suffer in body and spirit, and give us the desire to become holy and to be saints.

Fr. Thomas Rosica, CSB
CEO, Salt and Light Catholic Media Foundation
Former National Director and CEO, World Youth Day 2002

1

JOHN PAUL II:
THE STORY OF THE MAN

Karol Józef Wojtyla was born in the Polish town of Wado-wice, a small city 50 kilometres from Krakow, on May 18, 1920. He was the youngest of three children born to Karol Wojtyla and Emilia Kaczorowska. His mother died in 1929. His elder brother, Edmund, a doctor, died in 1932, and his father, a non-commissioned army officer, died in 1941. A sister, Olga, had died before young Karol was born.

Baptized on June 20, 1920, in the parish church of Wado-wice by Fr. Franciszek Zak, Karol made his First Holy Commun-ion at age nine and was confirmed at eighteen. Upon graduation from Marcin Wadowita Secondary School in Wadowice, he enrolled in Krakow's Jagiellonian University in 1938 and in a school for drama.

Nazi occupation forces closed the university in 1939 and Karol, now nineteen, had to work in a quarry (1940–1944) and then in the Solvay chemical factory to earn his living and to avoid being deported to Germany. In 1942, aware of his call to the priesthood, he began courses in the clandestine seminary of Krakow, run by Cardinal Adam Stefan Sapieha, Archbishop of Krakow. At the same time, Karol was one of the pioneers of the underground "Rhapsodic Theatre."

After the Second World War, Karol continued his studies in the reopened major seminary of Krakow and in the Faculty of Theology of Jagiellonian University. He was ordained to the priesthood by Cardinal Sapieha in Krakow on November 1, 1946. Shortly afterwards, Cardinal Sapieha sent him to Rome, where he worked under the guidance of the French Dominican Fr. Réginald Garrigou-Lagrange. He finished his doctorate in theology in 1948 with a thesis on the subject of faith in the works of Saint John of the Cross, *Doctrina de fide apud Sanctum Ioannem a Cruce*. At that time, during his vacations, he did pastoral ministry among Polish immigrants from France, Belgium and Holland.

In 1948, he returned to Poland and served as associate pastor of various parishes in Krakow, as well as chaplain to university students. This lasted until 1951, when he again took up his studies in philosophy and theology. In 1953, he defended a thesis on "Evaluation of the Possibility of Founding a Catholic Ethic on the Ethical System of Max Scheler" at the Catholic University of Lublin. Later he became professor of moral theology and social ethics in the major seminary of Krakow and in the Faculty of Theology of Lublin.

On July 4, 1958, Karol was appointed titular bishop of Ombi and auxiliary of Krakow by Pope Pius XII, and was consecrated on September 28, 1958, in Wawel Cathedral, Krakow, by Archbishop Eugeniusz Baziak. On January 13, 1964, he was installed as Archbishop of Krakow by Pope Paul VI, who made him a cardinal on June 26, 1967. Besides participating in the sessions of the Second Vatican Council (1962–1965), where he made an important contribution to the Pastoral Constitution of the Church in the Modern World, *Gaudium et Spes*, Cardinal Wojtyla participated in all the assemblies of the Synods of Bishops.

On October 16, 1978, the College of Cardinals made a momentous choice and elected Karol Wojtyla pope. Affirming the ministry of his predecessors – John XXIII, Paul VI and John

Paul I – he took the name of John Paul II. On October 22, 1978, he solemnly and formally inaugurated his Petrine ministry as the 263rd successor to the Apostle. It was during the homily of this Mass that he would set before the world the mantra and refrain that would resound throughout his time as pope:

> Brothers and sisters, do not be afraid to welcome Christ and accept his power. Help the Pope and all those who wish to serve Christ and with Christ's power to serve the human person and the whole of mankind. Do not be afraid. Open wide the doors for Christ. To his saving power open the boundaries of States, economic and political systems, the vast fields of culture, civilization and development. Do not be afraid. Christ knows "what is in man". He alone knows it.

John Paul II's papacy was one of the longest in the history of the Church, lasting nearly 27 years. Driven by his pastoral care for all churches and by a sense of openness and charity to the entire human race, John Paul II exercised the Petrine ministry with a tireless missionary spirit, dedicating all his energies and life to it. He made 104 pastoral visits outside Italy, three of which were in Canada.

On April 2, 2005, at 9:37 p.m., the eve of the Second Sunday of Easter and Divine Mercy Sunday, this good and holy shepherd departed this world for the house of the Father. From that evening until the funeral Mass, well over three million pilgrims came to Rome to pay homage to the mortal remains of the pope. Some of them lined up for over 24 hours to enter St. Peter's Basilica and pray for a few seconds before his body. Finally, on April 8, John Paul II's body rested in St. Peter's Square one last time before millions of women and men. Deeply moved by his faithful witness and enduring hope, the throngs of crowds acclaimed throughout the funeral Mass, "*Santo subito* – Sainthood now!"

Perhaps in response to the people's cries on that windy and dreary day, Pope Benedict XVI, on April 28, 2005, broke with tradition and waived the normal five-year waiting period before beginning the cause of beatification and canonization for John Paul II. Two months later, the cause was officially opened on June 28, 2005, by Cardinal Camillo Ruini, Vicar General for the Diocese of Rome. Few could imagine that only eight years later, on Divine Mercy Sunday, another pope would inscribe Karol Józef Wojtyla – Pope John Paul II – into the Church's book of saints.

2

"A Pope from Galilee": Remembering Pope John Paul II

On a warm weekend in August 2004, as I worked in the Toronto studios of Salt and Light Catholic Television Network – a project very much inspired by John Paul II – two screens in our master control room were depicting two very different human dramas being played out on two world stages. One TV network was airing scenes of the Olympic Games from Athens, featuring and exalting the human body in its youthfulness, agility and beauty. Another monitor carried scenes unfolding at a famous Catholic shrine tucked away in the Pyrenees in southern France, featuring not sportsmanship and physical excellence, but diminishment, suffering, disfigurement and pain that are so much a part of the pilgrimage centre at Lourdes. The key actor in this moment of pathos was an 84-year-old pope, slumped over on his kneeler as he prayed before the image of the Mother of God who had appeared in Lourdes more than 150 years earlier.

The contrasting dramas on that August weekend struck me as unique teaching moments, offering the world some profound truths about living and dying, youthfulness and old age, and the cost of commitment and total self-giving. Athens and its glorious medallists come and go with the passage of time. Lourdes and its exceptional pilgrim engraved on the memories and hearts of pilgrims and viewers throughout the world the enduring gift of one's life to others. Like so many others who watched those images from Lourdes, I realized that John Paul II was beginning the final act of a brilliant 27-year ministry. He was an actor who knew the power of gesture and symbol, and allowed himself to be a kind of spectacle to the world.

Now that the struggle is over, the curtain fallen, the race won, the heavenly victory his, how do we characterize such a complex man? Too often it is in simplistic, political, literary or journalistic terms, in which we either praise or dismiss John Paul II as a pope with one word: "conservative," "dynamic," "politician," "Polish," "aging," "infirm," "incompetent," "dying." I think Pope John Paul II defies such a simple analysis. There are, however, some indications as to what kept him going, what motivated him, what were his dreams and passions. And why, of all things, did the young people of the world respond so positively to this elderly bishop who, in the final years, represented the opposite of the cult of the body and the myth of eternal youth, the opposite of the falsehood of rampant freedom without commitment and of love and sexuality without responsibility. He did not present young people with the hollow façade and quick sound bites of self-serving politicians, wealthy sports heroes and empty Hollywood personalities of our day. And the youth loved him for that.

I was a nineteen-year-old university student on October 16, 1978, when the cardinals of the Catholic Church elected Karol Wojtyla as the 263rd successor to the Apostle Peter. They called to Rome a man from a distant country, a youthful athlete who took the world and the Church by storm. At the time of John Paul II's election, André Frossard, a well-known French journalist, wrote: "This isn't a pope from Poland; this is a pope from Galilee." The press nicknamed him "God's athlete," and later "God's astronaut," because he travelled a distance equivalent to more than three times that between the earth and the moon over the course of 100 international trips – pastoral visits, as he called them. He fulfilled remarkably his role of "Successor of Peter" for 27 years. But even more than that, he was the "Successor of Paul," taking the Church off the banks of the Tiber River in Rome and bringing the Good News to the farthest corners of the earth.

For nearly 27 years, the eyes of the world were fixed on this Polish actor, philosopher, politician, theologian, pastor, prophet, mystic and poet. This world leader of a billion Catholics was the first pontiff of the media, satellite and Internet age. He had a commanding presence on centre stage. How many times did we smile in reading headlines such as "Pope installs swimming pool at Castel Gandolfo" or "Roman Pontiff hits ski slopes in the Abruzzi mountains" or "Wojtyla returns to Poland and hikes in his Tatra mountains" during one of his many trips back to his homeland?

How could we forget the extraordinary privilege that we Canadians had in hosting him on his last vacation in 2002, when Lake Simcoe, just north of Toronto, was called "Holy Sea" and the headlines read "Pope loves Strawberry Island Retreat," "John Paul II's love boat meets handicapped children at Huronia Regional Centre" or "Pope loves Sisters' Morrow Park in Toronto"? Through all of these moments, John Paul II lowered many of the Vatican's curtains of privacy and revealed to us secrets that had never been realized before: that popes are human and need to play and even have lunch with young people every now and then on islands in Canadian lakes.

Imagine the impact that such images had on young people! I know the impact they had on me. In fact, in the six times I visited with the pope after World Youth Day 2002, he would ask me, with a glimmer in his eye and a little smile, about Strawberry Island. I was no longer a Basilian Father but rather one of the "Padri dell'Isola," one of the "Fathers of the Island." Gone were the days in the Vatican when we Basilians were only known for our great academic pursuits and institutions across North America, and especially in Canada. With this pope, our island summer retreat left a lasting impression.

What kept him going and inspired him for the long haul? Besides his mystical faith in Christ, his love for the Church and his unwavering hope, it was young people. During a packed press conference at the National Trade Centre in Exhibition Place during World Youth Day 2002, one of the journalists from a major American network asked me publicly: "So what medication is the pope taking to stay alive?" Vatican officials told me to avoid such questions, but I took the microphone and a sudden rippled hush came over the hall. I responded: "There are two prescribed drugs: one is young people and the other is Strawberry Island." The people in the room roared with laughter, and the pope's Press Secretary leaned over to me and simply said: "Bravo. That's exactly it!"

3

A Pastor and a Brother:
1984 Visit to Canada

Pope John Paul II left Canada in 2002 very much as he had arrived – not as a head of state, but as a pastor and brother. The first pope to travel the vast landscape of our country, he first came in 1984, spending more time in Canada than in any other country outside of Italy. Upon his arrival in the Quebec City suburb of Sainte-Foy, in his Opening Address, John Paul II noted the tremendous journey he would embark upon: "In the next eleven days I shall cross your country from one ocean to the other, 'a mari usque ad mare.'" Regardless of the distance, he wished to keep his visit a humble one and to sit as a brother and friend. It was to be a time for him to ask questions of us and for us to ask questions of him.

With his arrival on September 9 in Quebec City, John Paul II began a 15,000-kilometre journey that took him from the Atlantic to the Pacific. When the visit ended on September 20, he had visited Quebec City, Trois-Rivières, Montreal, St. John's, Moncton, Halifax, Toronto, Midland (Ontario), Winnipeg–Saint Boniface, Edmonton, Yellowknife, Vancouver and Ottawa-Hull. In addition to these many cities, he visited notable Canadian shrines, such as Sainte-Anne-de-Beaupré, Cap-de-la-Madeleine, St. Joseph's Oratory and Martyrs' Shrine in Midland. Millions of Canadians turned out to greet the pontiff, to pray and celebrate with him, and many of us were deeply moved by his words and presence.

Speaking in English and in French, John Paul II made more than 30 major addresses as well as many other statements. He spoke of themes that he strongly supported throughout his nearly 27 years as Vicar of Christ on earth: solidarity, justice, peace, the place of youth, and Jesus Christ as a beacon of hope.

Even before landing in Canada in 1984, he sent a pre-recorded television message entitled "I Am Also Waiting to Meet You" that was transmitted across the country in preparation for his historic visit. That message was like an overture to the great themes that would resound across the country. Some words of that message still resound in many hearts and minds:

> Your devotion and attention as you prepare to receive me can only be a humbling experience for me. Nevertheless, what prevails in my heart is the desire to be among you soon. I am sure that the Lord will repay you a hundred fold for your efforts on my behalf. As we celebrate together our common faith, it will be a moment of joy, of wonder and even of surprise.

He was worth waiting for, and his words proved so true, for in and through John Paul II, who had visited Canada several times as cardinal, we encountered an immense community, a dynamic assembly of believers, a living Church.

Although 30 years have passed since John Paul II's first visit to Canada, his words continue to speak to us. As we look back, we discover that his voice was a prophetic voice, a witness to Jesus' presence among us in both spirit and in those who so often suffer injustice. Perhaps now, more than ever, his words hold an ever-deeper meaning and call us to live our faith more fully in all that we do.

John Paul II first challenged us, during his homily at Université Laval in Quebec City, to respond to Jesus' question to his disciples: "Who do you say that I am?" He insisted that for us to respond to Jesus' question, we must cultivate a faith that is "active and strong." Moreover, he reminded us that our faith "must become always more personal, more and more rooted in prayer and in the experience of the Sacraments; it must reach the living God, in his Son Jesus Christ the Saviour, through the help of the Holy Spirit, in the Church." Yet for that faith to truly become transformative, for us and for others, it must be a faith that is lived with joy. "This is the faith that you ought to deepen with joy, in order to live it and to bear witness to it in daily life and in the new realms of culture."

The next day, September 9, at the Marian shrine of Cap-de-la-Madeleine, John Paul II continued his meditations on faith. Preaching to the hundreds of women and men gathered at the Quebec shrine, he prayed that we might be like Mary, turning to Jesus and remaining ever faithful to him, even in the midst of our trials:

> And we, when we feel God is far away, when we do not understand his ways, when the cross hurts our shoulders and our heart, when we suffer for our faith, let us learn from our Mother about steadfastness of faith in every trial, let us learn how to find strength and courage in our unconditional commitment to Jesus Christ.

Our faith and relationship with God continued to figure prominently throughout John Paul II's visits to Quebec and Canada. At the beatification liturgy of Sister Marie-Léonie in Montreal on September 11 during that first visit, he passionately reminded us of the centrality of God in our lives and society. This was a theme that ran throughout his papacy. God is the very source of our life. Nothing other than God will ever satisfy or sustain us:

To replace God is an impossible task. Nothing can fill the emptiness of his absence, neither abundant material wealth – which does not satisfy the heart – nor easy and permissive lifestyles which do not quench our thirst for happiness – nor the exclusive search for success or power for their own sake – nor even technology which makes it possible to change the world but brings no real answer to the mystery of our destiny.

Already, even in those early years of his ministry, John Paul II was deeply conscious of the difficulties of materialism. Not just for us, but for others. Later that same day, he met with the youth of Montreal and once again confronted our dependence upon material wealth and technology. He challenged the youth:

Broaden your vision beyond your usual milieu and your own country. Your brothers and sisters in vast regions of the world are without even the necessities of life, wounded in their dignity and oppressed in their freedom and their faith. Christ loves all his own and he identifies lovingly with the poorest. May he share with you his love for all his brothers and sisters! May he help you to live in that true solidarity which crosses frontiers and overcomes prejudices!

John Paul II did not forget the hunger and injustice experienced by so many Canadians. While visiting with people in New Brunswick on September 13, he called attention to the injustice encountered by those throughout the Atlantic provinces as well as in other parts of the world: "It is a cruel paradox that many of you who could be engaged in the production of food are in financial distress here, while at the same time hunger, chronic malnutrition and the threat of starvation afflict millions of people elsewhere in the world." In his role as pastor and shepherd of God's people, John Paul II encouraged civil leaders and authorities "to work together to find appropriate solutions to the problems at hand, including a restructuring of the economy, so that human needs be put before mere financial gain." All of us, he believed, had a responsibility for all God's people, at home and afar.

After spending time in the eastern and Atlantic provinces of Canada, John Paul II began his journey westward. Before heading west, however, he visited Canada's largest city, Toronto. Amid the city's ever-growing business life, he reflected upon technology's contribution to the well-being of humanity. As in so many other of John Paul II's talks and homilies to us in his various journeys, we hear a prophetic voice and witness. Who could have imagined then that his words spoken 30 years ago on technology would continue to speak to us today?

Although not opposed to the advances of technology, John Paul II was deeply mindful of the dignity and importance of the human person. Any technological advance, he argued, was to be at the service of humanity and those who are marginalized. However, it could very well also impose further injustice upon those who suffer most:

> Technology has contributed so much to the well-being of humanity; it has done so much to uplift the human condition, to serve humanity, and to facilitate and perfect its work. And yet at times technology cannot decide the full

measure of its own allegiance: whether it is for humanity or against it. The same technology that has the possibility to help the poor sometimes even contributes to poverty, limits the opportunities for work and removes the possibility of human creativity. In these and other instances technology ceases to be the ally of the human person.

While in Toronto, the pope drew attention to Canada's multicultural heritage, blessing the cornerstone of the Slovak Byzantine Cathedral of the Transfiguration in Unionville, and recalling the support of Ukrainian Catholics in Canada. In fact, throughout his many stops, he made a point of putting a spotlight on the country's diverse ethnic and cultural reality.

Justice continued to be at the forefront of John Paul II's mind days later, when he visited the people of Alberta and celebrated Eucharist with them in Edmonton. Preaching on the Beatitudes, he pleaded for those of us in the wealthier northern regions of the Americas to be attentive to the needs of those living in the south. Recalling our unity with all of humanity and confronting the increasing individualism of the day, John Paul II reminded us that we, too, lack when our neighbour lacks:

> The human person lives in a community, in society. And with the community he shares hunger and thirst and sickness and malnutrition and misery and all the deficiencies that result therefrom. In his or her own person the human being is meant to experience the needs of others.

This was to become a theme that would repeat itself throughout his papacy, and those of his successors.

Despite his heartfelt intention to travel to Fort Simpson in the Northwest Territories on September 18 to meet with Aboriginal people, John Paul II was unable to go due to inclement weather. This was to be a burden that he would carry throughout the remainder of his time in Canada. However, he yearned to at least share a message with people of Denendeh, and so on September 18, he delivered a radio message to greet the people and to "render respectful homage to the beginnings of human society in this vast region of North America." John Paul II recalled the Church's commitment to the Aboriginal communities from the times of the first missionaries and expressed gratitude for the welcome those missionaries received. However, he was mindful, too, that "Whatever faults and imperfections they had, whatever mistakes were made, together with whatever harm involuntarily resulted, they are now at pains to repair." At the same time, he affirmed the Church's love for Aboriginal peoples and the great need for further reconciliation and peace:

> As I mentioned in Midland, the hour has come to bind up wounds, to heal all divisions. It is a time for forgiveness, for reconciliation and for a commitment to building new relationships. Once again in the words of Saint Paul: "Now is the favourable time; this is the day of salvation" (2 Cor 6:2).

At the end of his historic journey, John Paul II bade farewell to Canada with a very moving address on the tarmac in Ottawa on September 20. In his address, he shared that

> the visit that I have just completed has given me a better appreciation of the beauty and diversity of your country,

and of the generosity of your people. I have enjoyed our meetings, thanks to your characteristic openness and enthusiasm. I cannot speak now of all that I will keep in my heart; that goes beyond what can be expressed in a few words.

Deeply moved by the outpouring of faith, love and generosity shared with him, John Paul II praised the faith of Canadians and expressed his certainty that we are ready to bring about the good news of the gospel to all women and men, in every corner and place in society:

> Your fervour is the sign that the message of the Successor of Peter, who has come to bear witness to Jesus Christ, has found men and women ready to work for a new world. It is the sign that the Christians of this country have the Holy Spirit living within them – the Holy Spirit who infuses into our hearts the love of God, who strengthens us in hope and gives fullness to our faith.

4

"I Looked Forward to the Day": 1987 Visit to Canada

There was a deep sadness in John Paul II's heart upon his departure from Canada in 1984 because he had been unable to visit Fort Simpson. He promised that he would return, and he did so, three years later, following a pastoral visit to the United States. On Sunday, September 20, 1987, John Paul II finally arrived in Fort Simpson, to the effusive joy of the Aboriginal communities. At a Mass on that eventful day, he spoke with them and shared his joy to be with them at last:

> I wish to tell you how happy I am to be with you, *the native peoples of Canada,* in this beautiful land of Denendeh. I have come first from across the ocean and now from the United States to be with you, and I know that many of you have also come from far away – from the frozen Arctic, from the prairies, from the forests, from all parts of this vast and beautiful country of Canada.

Mindful of the people's rich roots in Canada and their noble appreciation of the goodness of creation, John Paul praised the Aboriginal people's commitment: "For untold generations, you the native peoples have lived in *a relationship of trust with the Creator,* seeing the beauty and the richness of the land as coming from his bountiful hand and as deserving wise use and conservation." He challenged them to remain true to their vocational witness:

> As native peoples you are faced with a supreme test: that of promoting the religious, cultural and social values that will uphold your human dignity and ensure your future well-being. Your sense of sharing, your understanding of human community rooted in the family, the highly valued

relationships between your elders and your young people, your spiritual view of creation which calls for responsible care and protection of the environment – all of these traditional aspects of your way of life need to be preserved and cherished.

As he had done on so many other journeys to other lands and cultures, John Paul once again extolled the goodness of the Aboriginal peoples' life, culture and traditions. His affirmation is a reminder to all of us, even today, of the vital importance of every culture and people to the good of all of humanity.

Although he was unable to visit Fort Simpson on his 1984 trip, it is inspiring and astounding to have witnessed him devote a single trip, a special journey, to the First Nations of Canada. His journey was symbolic of his special love, and the need for the Church, to care for those women and men so often marginalized and placed at the fringes of society. It is a reminder to us today of our own need to cherish and honour the many Aboriginal cultures and peoples of Canada, and to share in the rich appreciation of all God's creation. More than that, his 1987 visit was a pointed challenge to Canadian society to heal its long-troubled relationship with First Nations peoples and seek forgiveness.

5

"THE HOPE OF THE CHURCH AND OF THE WORLD": JOHN PAUL II AND YOUTH

Inaugurating his papal ministry on October 22, 1978, John Paul II told young people, "You are the hope of the Church and of the world. You are my hope." He always loved them, and he believed in ministry and presence to youth. In fact, he was on a canoe trip with young people when Pope Pius XII named him bishop in 1958. The external trappings of priesthood and the rank and administrative burdens of the episcopacy would not take him away from his beloved young people. He knew deep inside him that without a love for and presence to young people, the Church would have no future.

He wrote in his 1994 book, *Crossing the Threshold of Hope*:

Whenever I meet young people in my travels throughout the world, I wait first of all to hear what they want to tell me about themselves, about their society, about their Church. And I always point out: What I am going to say to you is not as important as what you are going to say to me. You will not necessarily say it to me in words; you will say it to me by your presence, by your song, perhaps by your dancing, by your skits, and finally by your enthusiasm.

This is a lesson that some of us in Church leadership and ministry should take to heart quickly if we seek to make the gospel relevant to future generations.

From the beginning of his papal ministry, he insisted on meeting young people whenever he visited Roman parishes or foreign countries. Building on a tradition begun by his predecessor, Paul VI, in the twilight years of his reign (1976), John Paul II invited hordes of young people to Rome in 1984 for the Jubilee Year of the Redemption. He invited them again in March 1985 for the International Year of Youth, and, on Palm Sunday of that year, he established World Youth Days as a permanent event. "No one invented the World Youth Days. It was the young people themselves who created them," John Paul II wrote in *Crossing the Threshold of Hope*. In fact, he first sought them out; they then discovered him. Most of the World Youth Days, including ours in Canada, have been something of a surprise for priests and bishops, in that they surpassed all our expectations.

John Paul II enjoyed an incredible popularity with young Catholics. At World Youth Day in Rome in 2000, he called the young people of the world his "joy and his crown." In July 2002 in Toronto, he showed us that he still felt this way. Today's young people are experiencing an extreme crisis of fatherhood. I am convinced that they flocked to him because for many of them, he was the father they never had and the grandfather who had been so painfully absent in their lives. John Paul II was a rock, a moral compass and a very demanding friend. He made all of us discover our youthfulness, generosity and joy as he invited us to become salt and light in a world, a society and a culture that are so cynical and so often devoid of the flavour and joy of the gospel and the light and hope of Christ.

During the 17th World Youth Day's concluding Mass at Downsview Park in Toronto on Sunday, July 28, 2002, the pope spoke deeply personal and touching words to the assembled crowd of over 850,000 people:

> You are young and the pope is old and a bit tired. But he still fully identifies with your hopes and aspirations. Although

I have lived through much darkness, under harsh totalitarian regimes, I have seen enough evidence to be unshakably convinced that no difficulty, no fear is so great that it can completely suffocate the hope that springs eternal in the hearts of the young. Do not let that hope die! Stake your lives on it! We are not the sum of our weaknesses and failures; we are the sum of the Father's love for us and our real capacity to become the image of his son.

Nowhere was John Paul's faith in young people and personal tenacity more in evidence than on June 6, 2004, during his visit to Bern, Switzerland. He needed young people more than ever on that visit. Before he arrived in Switzerland, some 40 priests and lay leaders signed an open letter suggesting that the pope resign because of age and poor health. The sentiments were quite different in a Bern ice arena.

Pope John Paul II struggled in vain to proclaim the first sentence of his speech. After he had made three attempts to get the words out of his mouth, the 13,000 young people applauded in encouragement. At the same time, a monsignor approached him as if to take the microphone and let someone else read the speech. The pope slapped away the aide's hand and grabbed the mike back himself – and the crowd erupted in delight. John Paul the actor played with the crowd, egging them on. Then he read his speech without stopping.

At that event in Bern, the pope managed not only to talk but also to communicate, something that many healthy and younger Church leaders are unable to do! The crowd reacted to the content of the speech, giving the pope one of his biggest cheers when he recalled that he, too, was their age a long time ago. They applauded wildly with understanding when he told them Christianity was not an ideology, a book or a system, but above all the person of Christ.

The Swiss youth, and the millions watching the event on television, caught the poignancy when the pope, speaking of his own life, said it was a beautiful thing to be able to "give oneself to the very end for the cause of the kingdom of God." And they went wild when the pope, at the end of his speech, pronounced in a voice that was firm and clear as a bell: "Christ is speaking to you. Listen to him." Then the crowd was treated to another glimpse of papal tenacity, watching as the pope reprimanded his bishop secretary and, gesticulating with his fist, told him to bring the microphone back. He wanted to say goodbye in German, French and Italian, three of the four languages of Switzerland. What energy he gave to "his dear young friends" that day. What incredible energy and encouragement they gave to him! What an amazing role model he was for them. The relationship was mutual.

It's not remarkable that the pope saw his youthful friends as a metaphor of renewal and hope; what's remarkable is that the young people have seen and understood themselves that way as well. Very few leaders have ever had such an impact on young people as this leader has had. What will be the enduring messages and legacy of John Paul II on the young people who consider themselves to be part of the "John Paul II generation"? I consider myself part of that generation. The pope himself often said, "In the designs of Providence, there are no mere coincidences." Maybe the reason this man became pope is that he bore messages the world and especially young people needed to hear.

Let us consider six key aspects of Pope John Paul II's ministry and impact on young people.

First was the message and centrality of the radiant splendour of Jesus Christ as the unique Lord and Saviour of all. In order to be authentic believers, we must have a deep personal relationship with Jesus. Christianity, Catholicism, the sacraments are not courses, things, ideas, passing fancies, symbols – they are a person and his name is Jesus. He must be at the core of everything we are and do. Everything must begin anew from him.

Second was human dignity. In speaking of John Paul II several years ago, US President George W. Bush, one of the Pope's admirers, said:

> A young seminarian, Karol Wojtyla, saw the swastika flag flying over the ramparts of Wawel Castle … He shared the suffering of his people and was put into forced labour. From this priest's experience and faith came a vision: that every person must be treated with dignity, because every person is known and loved by God.

John Paul II impressed upon the new generation the dignity and sacredness of human life, from the earliest moments to its final moments. Life is an extraordinary adventure, a God-given gift to be cherished, treasured and protected. In John Paul II's "Culture of Life," we must make room for the stranger and the homeless. We must comfort and care for the sick and dying. We must look after the aged and the abandoned. We must welcome the immigrant. We must defend innocent children waiting to be born.

Third, John Paul II helped us to realize that the Church is dying in politically correct places where the gospel is preached as merely a lifestyle option in a global supermarket of spiritualities without the obligation of belonging to the Church. The Church is thriving where the full gospel is preached in clarity, charity, piety and devotion – in its full integrity. John Paul II told young people that there is every reason for the truth of the cross to be called the good news. Young people took these words to heart and have carried the cross around the world for the past 29 years. Not just the two beams of wood, but the message of the cross and its saving power. Here in Canada, we are unlikely to forget the powerful images of the World Youth Day cross on its historic sixteen-month, 43,000-kilometre pilgrimage from sea to sea to sea. The pope entrusted this cross to young people. They have carried it triumphantly across the face of the earth almost like an Olympic torch.

Fourth, John Paul II taught us that the adventure of orthodoxy – the challenge of fidelity and integrity, authenticity and solidarity – is what attracts young people today. They don't want to live on the surface. In a world that constantly panders to the young, a challenging Church, which combines the truth with charity and pastoral care, is a very attractive proposition. How many times did John Paul II remind young people that the family is the privileged place for the humanization of the person and of society, and that the future of the world and of the Church passes through it?

Fifth, John Paul II issued a clarion call to commitment. To his young friends he said: "Many and enticing are the voices that call out to you from all sides: many of these voices speak to you of a joy that can be had with money, success, and power. Mostly they propose a joy that comes with the superficial and fleeting pleasure of the senses." The alternative call was Jesus' siren song. "He calls you to be the salt and light of the world, to live in justice, to become instruments of love and peace." The choice was stark, self-denying, life defining, irrevocable. It was between "good and evil, between light and darkness, between life and death." There were no shortcuts or compromises for John Paul II, only clarity. And that is what the young are seeking today – not quick answers, but gospel clarity.

Finally, Pope John Paul II devoted the first major teaching project of his pontificate – 129 short talks between September of 1979 and November of 1984 – to providing a profoundly beautiful vision of human embodiment and erotic love. He gave this project the working title "Theology of the Body." Far from being a footnote to the Christian life, the way we understand the body and the sexual relationship concerns the whole Bible. It plunges us into the perspective of the whole gospel, of the whole teaching – even more, of the whole mission of Christ. Christ's mission, according to the spousal analogy of the Scriptures, is to "marry" us. He invites us to live with him in an eternal life-giving union of love. By helping us understand this profound interconnection between sex and the Christian mystery, John Paul's theology of the body not only paves the way for lasting renewal of marriage and the family; it also enables everyone to rediscover the meaning of the whole of existence, the meaning of life.

How many people are no longer afraid because they saw a pope who was not afraid! How many young seminarians and religious have spoken their "yes" because of him! How many young couples have made permanent commitments in marriage because of his profound theology of the body! How many ordinary people have done extraordinary things because of his influence, his teaching and his gestures!

6

"SALT FOR THE EARTH AND LIGHT FOR THE WORLD": WORLD YOUTH DAY 2002

One of John Paul's final moments of dedication and commitment to youth was in July 2002, when Toronto hosted the 17th International World Youth Day. Several hundred thousand young people from 172 nations descended upon the city – and with them came the elderly and infirm Pope John Paul II. Toronto may have lost the Olympic bid two years earlier, but it struck gold with World Youth Day, which I was privileged to serve as its National Director and Chief Executive Officer. The sheer numbers of people taking part in the four days of events astounded us. More than 350,000 people packed Exhibition Place on Thursday afternoon, July 25, for the opening ceremony with Pope John Paul II.

The following evening, Toronto's majestic University Avenue was transformed into the Via Dolorosa of Jerusalem as more than half a million people took part in the ancient Stations of the Cross. The Canadian Broadcasting Corporation/ Radio Canada told us that the worldwide television audience that night was more than a billion people in 160 countries.

The spectacular Saturday evening candlelight vigil at Downsview Park drew together more than 600,000 people, and the concluding papal mass on Sunday, with its atmospheric special effects, gathered 850,000 people at a former military base in the city. Even the most cynical among us could not help but be impressed, even moved, by the streams of young people who expressed their joy at being Christians in a complex and wartorn world.

On the tarmac for the Saturday evening vigil, John Paul II spoke to the young people: "The new millennium opened with two contrasting scenarios," he declared.

One, the sight of multitudes of pilgrims coming to Rome during the Great Jubilee to pass through the Holy Door which is Christ, our Savior and Redeemer; and the other, the terrible terrorist attack on New York, an image that is a sort of icon of a world in which hostility and hatred seem to prevail. The question that arises is dramatic: On what foundations must we build the new historical era that is emerging from the great transformations of the 20th century? Is it enough to rely on the technological revolution now taking place, which seems to respond only to criteria of productivity and efficiency, without reference to the individual's spiritual dimension or to any universally shared ethical values? Is it right to be content with provisional answers to the ultimate questions, and to abandon life to the impulses of instinct, to short-lived sensations or passing fads?

The provocative images the pope evoked that night remain engraved on people's memories. In fact, throughout the pope's messages delivered to us during those blessed days, he touched upon all that had challenged us in our two-year preparation period. During the Angelus prayer at Downsview Park that Sunday, July 28, before the 850,000 gathered and a worldwide television audience of many millions, John Paul II summed up beautifully the sentiments of countless people who were touched in some way by World Youth Day 2002: "As we prepare to return home, I say, in the words of Saint Augustine: 'We have been happy together in the light we have shared. We have really enjoyed being together. We have really rejoiced. But as we leave one another, let us not leave Him.'"

Rome had its Tor Vergata, Cologne had its Marienfeld, Australia had its Randwick Racecourse, and Madrid its Cuatro Vientos. But we had our Exhibition Place and Downsview Park. We also had September 11, massive economic collapse and political upheaval in many of the South American countries that were to send us thousands of young people. We had the constant uncertainty of whether the physically fragile pope would be able to make the trip. And when it was finally decided that there would be a *habemus Papam* in Toronto, the Vatican also announced two other papal journeys attached to ours: Guatemala and Mexico City!

During that preparatory year of 2001–2002, North America also experienced the moral earthquake of January 2002, when the clergy sexual abuse scandal erupted and threatened our event to the very core. I have never prayed as much as I did from October 2001 to July 2002. Our final event was graced with an electrical storm of truly biblical proportions on the early morning of July 28. Against this backdrop, we heard our challenge in Canada – to recover the depth, beauty and vastness of the Church's mission.

Canada and Toronto needed World Youth Day to call us back to our deeply Christian origins and heritage. It is only when a nation and a society reclaim their original identity that they can ever hope to become authentically multicultural, tolerant and open to others.

What we learned from World Youth Day 2002

Twelve years after the great event of Toronto in 2002, we are taking stock of the gifts we received, asking how the vision and hope of John Paul II have influenced our own efforts in pastoral ministry with young people. The experiences of World Youth Days in recent years have brought much new life to each of the countries where the great events have taken place. One of the important goals of World Youth Day is to instill hope and vibrancy in the Church – to challenge the cynicism, despair and meaninglessness so prevalent in the world today. Pope John Paul II knew well that our world today overflows with fragmentation, loneliness, alienation and rampant globalization that exploit the poor.

What did the joy, exuberance and creativity surrounding the 2002 World Youth Day teach us, and how did they transform youth and young adult ministry in the Canadian Church? How have we initiated a "preferential option" for young people in the Church today? How can we give the flavour of the gospel and the light of Christ to the world today? Let us consider seven aspects of World Youth Days.

1. Biblical theme

Pope John Paul's biblical theme for WYD 2002 was providential and highly appropriate for our Canadian society and a world steeped in mediocrity and darkness: "You are the salt of the earth. You are the light of the world" (Matthew 5:13-14). During World Youth Days, bishops and cardinals serve as teachers and catechists. Thousands of young people gather around them to hear reflections based on the Word of God, and in particular on the theme of the event. This novel invention has taken on a life of its own, becoming an intrinsic part of the celebrations. How many times was this evoked during recent

Synods of Bishops in Rome on "The Word of God" and "The New Evangelization"? The catechetical teaching sessions on Scripture have become not only a unique encounter between generations, but also an opportunity to proclaim and preach the Word of God across cultures, offering to young people concrete possibilities for living a biblically rooted life.

2. Liturgies

World Youth Days offer deeply prayerful celebrations of the Eucharist as well as opportunities to experience the Eucharistic Lord in moments of quiet prayer, adoration, and communal and individual worship. The liturgies of World Youth Day are prepared and planned with great diligence, care, precision and tremendous beauty. Through these moments, young people are offered privileged moments of encounter with Jesus himself. These moments are enhanced by the careful selection of liturgical music that is not in competition with the world of theatre, spectacle and the surrounding din of noise and emptiness.

3. The sacrament of Reconciliation

During WYD 2002 in Toronto, over 100,000 young people celebrated the sacrament of Reconciliation. Through this sacrament, Christ lets us meet him and brings out the best in us. This sacrament is a privileged encounter with Christ, who heals, forgives and liberates us.

4. Devotions

World Youth Days offer the Church profound moments where we can deepen our Christian piety and devotion. In Canada during 2001–2002, the historic 43,000-kilometre pilgrimage of the World Youth Day cross and the powerful presentation of the Stations of the Cross were a provocative, profound witness of the Christian story in the heart of a modern city. I and many others were convinced that even if, for some reason, the World Youth Day event itself had to be cancelled because of the impact of September 11, the pilgrimage of the cross had already worked its miracles across our vast land and had united the Church in ways that nothing before it was ever able to do.

One year after World Youth Day 2002 had ended, the ever-colourful, rather comical Jewish mayor of the huge city of Toronto called a press conference to announce that he would no longer seek political office after 43 years of public service. At that memorable gathering, with hordes of journalists and media moguls in attendance, Mayor Mel Lastman stood at the podium with a person on either side of him: his rabbi and me, whom he called publicly "my priest." In his farewell speech to the crowd that day, he said: "The crowning moment of my political career was on a Friday night last July, on the main boulevard of downtown Toronto, during the Jesus parade." (He never quite got the term for the Stations of the Cross right.) The mayor then told the assembly: "That was the night that God claimed the city for his own."

5. Holiness

During his pontificate, John Paul II proclaimed 1,338 blesseds and 482 saints. Young adults need heroes and heroines today, and the pope gave us outstanding models of holiness and humanity. Nine young blesseds and saints were patrons of

WYD 2002; several more were patrons for WYD 2005. Pope Benedict XVI spoke to that great assembly of over one million young people gathered in prayer at Marienfeld in 2005, exclaiming: "The saints ... are the true reformers. Now I want to express this in an even more radical way: only from the saints, only from God does true revolution come, the definitive way to change the world."

6. Vocations

One of the significant contributions of World Youth Day 2002 to the universal Church and to young people across the globe was the highly successful Vocations Pavilion at Exhibition Place. The security personnel informed us that 50,000 to 55,000 young people visited the pavilion each day for the week of World Youth Day 2002. The Australians built on our tradition with their highly successful Vocations Pavilion at World Youth Day 2008.

The phenomenon of World Youth Days has become a powerful seedbed for vocations to the priesthood, consecrated life and lay ecclesial ministries. Whether it is because those who have already sensed a call choose to attend World Youth Days out of their strong faith life, or because the events awaken young adults for the first time to the special call of God, World Youth Days can be a moment of life-changing discernment.

Over the past twelve years, I have received many letters, messages and testimonies from young people speaking convincingly that their vocations were born at large vigil ceremonies with John Paul II, during the sacrament of Reconciliation at World Youth Days, and in the midst of catechesis sessions. A whole new generation of young people identifies the World Youth Day experiences as critical in their discernment process. In working with Catholic young adults, we have the responsibility and obligation to raise the subject of priestly, religious and lay ministry vocations with openness, conviction, pastoral sensitivity and common sense.

7. Openness to young people's views

I like to refer to this point as "overcoming the crisis of ideologies" that has plagued my generation and several others. Excessive tensions arising from Church politics, gender issues, liturgical practices, language and false interpretations of the Second Vatican Council – all of these influence today's candidates for ordained ministry, religious life and pastoral involvement in the Church. The grumblings, discontent, cynicism, fatigue, unfair labelling and pigeonholing of others, the lack of charity and lack of hope of my generation and older generations rise to fever pitch, keeping us blinded to a new generation of young people who might be much more serious about Church, God and discipleship of Jesus than we are. Many of my generation do not wish to admit this fact.

The great tragedy today is that many people in leadership positions in the Church, in religious life and in "professional" pastoral ministry are out of touch with the younger generation. Ideologues have the ability to silence others with blanket statements, especially when it comes to vocational discernment and loving Christ and the Church. How many times have I heard university chaplains, vocation directors, formation directors and youth ministers express fears and even disdain over the pious and devotional practices of today's generation of young people? Such piety and devotion are not to be downplayed or dismissed in vocational and priestly formation work. They can indeed become a creative foundation upon which we can build for the future. Piety and devotion can be springboards to mature faith.

World Youth Day does not belong to one pope

In remarks at the concluding Mass of Australia's 2008 World Youth Day, Sydney's Cardinal George Pell, thanking Pope Benedict XVI, said that World Youth Day acts as an antidote to images of Catholicism as being in decline or wracked by controversy: "It shows the Church as it really is, alive with evangelical energy." Cardinal Pell concluded his address to Pope Benedict XVI at Randwick Racecourse with these prophetic and affirming words:

> Your Holiness, the World Youth Days were the invention of Pope John Paul the Great. The World Youth Day in Cologne was already announced before your election. You decided to continue the World Youth Days and to hold this one in Sydney. We are profoundly grateful for this decision, indicating that the World Youth Days do not belong to one pope, or even one generation, but are now an ordinary part of the life of the Church. The John Paul II generation – young and old alike – is proud to be faithful sons and daughters of Pope Benedict.

World Youth Day in reflection

World Youth Day 2002 in Toronto was not a show, a rave party, a protest or photo opportunity. It was an invitation and a proposal for something new. Against a global background of terror and fear, economic collapse in many countries and ecclesial scandals, World Youth Day 2002 presented a bold, alternative vision of compelling beauty, hope and joy … a vision and energy.

We may choose to speak of our World Youth Days as something in the past – events that brightened the shadows and monotony of our lives at one shining moment in history in 2002 in Toronto, or 2008 in Sydney, or 2013 in Rio. Some may wish to call those golden days "Camelot" moments. That is one way to consider World Youth Day – fading memories of extraordinary moments in Canadian, Australian and Brazilian history.

There is, however, another way: the gospel way. The gospel story is not about "Camelot" but about "Magnificat," constantly inviting Christians to take up Mary's hymn of praise and thanksgiving for the ways that Almighty God breaks through human history here and now. This way is not only nourished by memories, however good and beautiful they may be. The resurrection of Jesus is not a memory of a distant, past event; it is good news that continues to be fulfilled today – here and now. The Christian story is neither folklore nor nostalgia – not merely a trip down triumphal Church Lane.

As we continue to bask in the glorious light of the summer of 2002 in Canada, we must be honest and admit that World Youth Days offer no panacea or quick fix to the problems and challenges of our times, or the challenges facing the Church today as we reach out to younger generations. Instead, World

Youth Days offer a new framework and new lenses through which we look at the Church and the world, and build our common future. One thing is clear: no one could go away from Toronto 2002 thinking that it is possible to compartmentalize the faith or reduce it to a few rules and regulations and Sunday observances.

World Youth Day 2002 and the visit of Pope John Paul II brought Toronto not gold, silver and bronze medals, but something even greater: it gave Canada its soul. Through those blessed days, we experienced once again the fulfillment of the Second Vatican Council's desires: together we were witnesses to the Council's hopes and dreams for the Church and for humanity, when every nation, every tribe, came together to worship the Lord. We received the power from on high to be a light unto the world (Acts 1:8)! Now let us pray together that the John Paul II and Benedict XVI and Francis generations will truly become the Spirit's joyful witnesses to the ends of the earth – that they may truly become Catholic, universal, open to the world.

7

READING THE SIGNS OF THE TIMES: CHALLENGES FOR THE CHURCH IN CANADA

Throughout his nearly 27-year pontificate, Pope John Paul II brought about a clear change in the image of the papacy itself. The pope and the Roman Curia – his ministry – is not simply the "home office" on the banks of the Tiber in Rome. There are few places on this planet that have not been touched by Pope John Paul II. Through his pastoral visits – 104 international and 145 diocesan in Italy – the Holy Father went to the local churches, confirming them in the apostolic faith that they are part of a great communion of charity. Who can forget the powerful images of the Holy Father's visit to this vast country in 1984, 1987 and 2002? From Vancouver to Newfoundland, from the First Nations longhouse in Midland to the origins of the Church in Quebec, the Holy Father crisscrossed this vast land from sea to sea. He is the Successor of Peter, but also the Successor of Paul, the missionary of the gospel.

John Paul II tirelessly travelled the world, bringing to women and men of every race, nation and culture a message of hope: that human dignity is rooted in the fact that each human being is created in the image and likeness of God. The Holy Father's courageous and steadfast witness to the power of the Risen Lord has been the hallmark of his pontificate, in which he has opened wide the doors of many human hearts and of many nations to Christ. By his witness and preaching of the Catholic faith, John Paul II has played a key role in changing the course of history.

1. Deepen the Church's relationship with the universal Church

The first challenge to the Church in Canada is *to deepen its relationship with the living communion of faith of the whole*

Church. Canada has much from its experience to offer to the universal Church – things like tolerance, peace, social justice, a rich heritage of saints and blesseds who brought us the faith. That is the mission of the Church in Canada as well. We cannot forget the deeply Christian roots and heritage of this country. This is not only a religious question but also an anthropological one, since human identity cannot be separated or divorced from its Christian identity. In an increasingly secularized world, the place and role of religion in our cultural identity must be re-evaluated and revitalized. There can be no future without a past. Our present has been formed by the Christian heritage handed down to us; we must ensure that future generations have a similar Christian heritage to hand on.

2. Uphold the dignity of the human person

When he entered the Second Vatican Council as Bishop Karol Wojtyla, the Holy Father realized that one of the primary tasks of the Council would be to address the wounds caused to humanity by the twin totalitarian evils of Nazism and Communism, both of which he experienced firsthand in Poland. The 20th century had shown new depths of the debasement of humanity.

For John Paul II, Jesus Christ is both the answer and the goal of humanity. Christ is the only redeemer of the human family. Thus, in 1959, as a young Polish bishop, he submitted a paper to the preparatory commission for the Second Vatican Council contending that the crisis of humanism at the midpoint of a century that prided itself on humanism should be the organizing principle for the Council's deliberation. The Church did not exist for itself. There was much talk before and during the Council of "reading the signs of the times," yet here was a bishop who had put his finger on the deepest question of the century: that of creating a humanism adequate to the aspirations of the men and women of the age. This was truly the joy and hope of Vatican II.

Through his extraordinary and mystical faith, born from his own experiences, he has given to the Church and humanity a great hope. His own physical suffering during his latter years reminded us that there are no disposable human beings. Even in his suffering and infirmity, he offered to the world a powerful testimony of human dignity.

Thus, this second challenge to the Church in Canada is *to uphold and to protect the great dignity and value of human life, from its first moment to its final moment,* and to recognize the primary place of human life – the family. God's most precious gift is the gift of human life, which is uniquely expressed in the life of each human being, a life that comes to its full fruition in the family. The family is the place where a person first receives his or her humanity. It is the family that first educates us as human beings. It is the family that first introduces us to the realities of our existence in this world.

The Church must offer to the world the Gospel of Life and the Culture of Life in all of its simplicity and beauty. In doing so, we advance the brilliant vision of Pope John Paul II, who offered to us a joyful and hopeful humanism that is the heart of the message of the Second Vatican Council.

3. Form laity and priests for ministry

As shepherd and teacher of the universal Church, John Paul II brought to a conclusion the bold teaching and vision of the Second Vatican Council. He gave it an authoritative interpretation and taught us courageously that Jesus Christ is the ultimate truth and the answer to the deepest longings of the human person.

At the third session of the Second Vatican Council in 1964, as Archbishop Wojtyla, he entered the debate on a proposed decree on the apostolate of the laity. He thought that a zealous, educated laity was essential if Christian humanism was to penetrate all of society, especially in those places where priests cannot easily go. He recommended a "dialogue" between clergy and laity for their mutual enrichment in pursuit of their common purpose. For nearly 27 years he lived that dialogue on a daily basis in his conversations, meetings, encounters and audiences with millions of lay people.

The third challenge to the Church in Canada is *in the area of formation of the laity and preparation of priests for ministry in the Church.* We must both avoid at all costs a clericalization of the laity and a laicization of the clergy in our formation and educational programs. Lay people must be formed into the art of evangelizing culture, penetrating all of those places where the clergy may never reach: the workplace, the board room, places where decisions are made that will affect the future of humanity. All of our educational programs must introduce people to holiness and union with God, the final goal of our efforts, and to the radiant figure of Jesus Christ. We must preserve the

uniqueness and distinctiveness of ordained ministry, and offer concrete proposals of collaboration with lay people to our
young people preparing for ordained ministry.

4. Keep alive the spirit of World Youth Day

Pope John Paul II was the great Christian witness of our
time to young and old, to rich and poor, to the powerful and the
humble. Following the example of Jesus Christ, he always called
for a special love for the poor and defenceless, especially in the
developing world, and reminded us to be united in solidarity.

The fourth challenge to the Church in Canada is *to keep
alive the memory of World Youth Day 2002 and act upon it.* New
structures for young adult ministry, university chaplaincy and
promoting vocations must be put in place to respond to the
new awareness of Christ and the Church that is born through
the universal dynamic of World Youth Day 2002. I believe that
there is a lot of generosity to be discovered among the young
people of Canada.

5. Renew our Marian piety and popular religious traditions

A distinctive Marian thread ran through the life and
ministry of John Paul II. Long before his episcopal and papal
motto *Totus Tuus* ("totally yours") were made known to the
world, Mary was present in the life of Karol Wojtyla. His parish
church in Wadowice contained a side chapel dedicated to Our
Lady of Perpetual Help. In the mornings, the secondary school
students would make a visit to the chapel before classes began.
After classes, in the afternoon, many students would go there

to pray to the Blessed Virgin. Also, on a hilltop in Wadowice stood a Carmelite monastery dating back to the time of Saint Raphael Kalinowski (1835–1907). People from Wadowice would go there in great numbers, and this was reflected in the widespread use of the scapular of Our Lady of Mount Carmel. John Paul II would speak about having received the scapular, at the age of ten. He still wore it as pope.

His devotion to Mary took shape from his early childhood and adolescence up through secondary school. When he was in Krakow, in Debniki, he joined the "Living Rosary" group in the Salesian parish. There was a special devotion there to Mary, Help of Christians. In Debniki, when his priestly vocation was developing, under the influence of Jan Tyranowski, a change took place in his understanding of devotion to the Mother of God. The young Karol was already convinced that Mary leads us to Christ, but he slowly began to realize that Christ leads us to his Mother.

During the Second World War, while Karol was employed as a factory worker, his Marian devotion deepened and matured. Over time, he realized that true devotion to the Mother of God is actually Christocentric; indeed, it is profoundly rooted in the Blessed Trinity and in the mysteries of the Incarnation and redemption. It was during those days that he was greatly assisted by a book of Saint Louis-Marie Grignion de Montfort, entitled *A Treatise on the True Devotion to the Blessed Virgin*. He learned that Mary brings us closer to Christ and leads us to him, provided that we live her mystery in Christ.

Toward the end of his life, in his Apostolic Letter *Rosarium Virginis Mariae* (Rosary of the Virgin Mary), John Paul II wrote, "It would be impossible to name all the many saints who discovered in the Rosary a genuine path to holiness. We need but mention Saint Louis-Marie Grignion de Montfort, the author of an excellent work on the Rosary called 'The Secret of the Rosary'." He continues:

> This is the luminous principle expressed by the Second Vatican Council which I have so powerfully expressed in my own life and have made the basis of my episcopal motto: Totus Tuus. This motto is of course inspired by the teaching of Saint Louis Marie Grignion de Montfort, who explained in the following words Mary's role in the process of our configuration to Christ: "Our entire perfection consists in being conformed, united and consecrated to Christ."

The fifth challenge to the Church in Canada is *to develop, renew, our Marian piety, popular religious traditions in light of the gospels, the Second Vatican Council, and the teaching and example of Pope John Paul II.* By breathing into these ancient, sacred traditions new life, new understandings of Scripture, theology and tradition, we renew the faith of God's people and of the entire Church.

In 2003, in his very moving homily in St. Peter's Square during the 25th Anniversary Mass of his Pontificate, he shared with the world his own fear and trepidation during that night when the Lord asked him to accept such a great responsibility and burden. He turned to divine mercy in order to answer the question "Do you accept?" With confidence he replied:

"In the obedience of the faith, before Christ my Lord, entrusting myself to the Mother of Christ and of the Church, aware of the great difficulties, I accept." This is why, from the very first day, I have never ceased to urge people: "Do not be afraid to welcome Christ and accept his power!"

8

THE SUFFERING AND DEATH OF A SHEPHERD: WHAT JOHN PAUL II TAUGHT US AT THE END

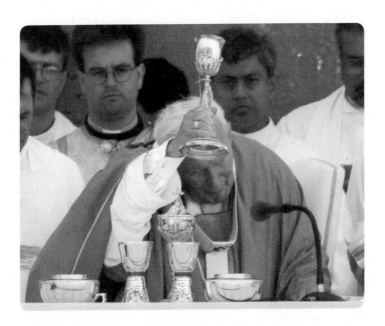

One of the most profound lessons John Paul II taught us in the twilight of his pontificate was that everyone must suffer, even the Vicar of Christ. Rather than hide his infirmities, as most public figures do, he let the whole world see what he went through. The passing of John Paul II did not take place in private, but before television cameras and the whole world. In the final act of his life, the athlete was immobilized; the distinctive, booming voice silenced; the hand that produced voluminous encyclicals no longer able to write. John Paul II's final homily was an icon of his Galilean Master's final words to Simon Peter:

> Very truly, I tell you, when you were younger, you used to fasten your own belt and to go wherever you wished. But when you grow old, you will stretch out your hands, and someone else will fasten a belt around you and take you where you do not wish to go." … After this [Jesus] said to him, "Follow me." (John 21:18-19)

One of the infrequently cited writings of John Paul II is his 1984 Apostolic Letter *Salvifici Doloris* (On the Christian Meaning of Human Suffering). The late pope, following the Apostle Paul and the entire Catholic Tradition, maintained throughout his life that it is precisely in suffering that Christ displayed his solidarity with humanity, and in which we can grow in solidarity with Christ, who is our life.

As he writes in *Salvifici Doloris*, suffering is the consequence of sin, and Christ embraces that consequence, rather than repudiating it. By embracing suffering, he shares fully in it; he takes the consequence of sin into and onto himself. He does this out of love for us, not simply because he wants to redeem us, but because he wants to be with us, to share what we share, to experience what we experience. And it is this shared love, this shared suffering in love, that completes and perfects the relationship broken in sin, and so redeems us.

Pope John Paul II taught us that the meaning of suffering is fundamentally changed by the Incarnation. Apart from the Incarnation, suffering is the consequence of sin. It offers opportunities for insight into oneself, for personal growth and for demonstrating practical love for others; but these are incidental. Because of the Incarnation, however, we become sharers in the Body of Christ. Our suffering becomes his suffering and an expression of redeeming love.

Because he was the leader of a billion Catholics, because he was the first pontiff of the satellite and Internet age, reaching out to billions more, and because he was John Paul II, who led the Church for more than 26 years – in that public experience of suffering was found enormous power. And that he certainly knew. In 1981, after recovering from the gunshot wound that almost took his life in St. Peter's Square, John Paul declared that suffering, as such, is one of the most powerful messages in Christianity.

During the final years of his pontificate, John Paul II brought suffering back into the realm of the expected in human life. Everyone could see that his spirituality gave him an inner strength – a spirituality through which one can also overcome fear, even the fear of death. What an incredible lesson for the world! His struggle with the physical effects of aging was also a valuable lesson to a society that finds it hard to accept growing older.

In 1994, as age and infirmity began to incapacitate John Paul publicly, he told his followers that he had heard God and was about to change the way he led the Church. "I must lead her with suffering," he said. "The pope must suffer so that every family and the world should see that there is, I would say, a higher gospel: the gospel of suffering, with which one must prepare the future."

A letter to his peers

In 1999, in preparation for the Great Jubilee of 2000, Pope John Paul II published his Letter to the Elderly. Following his letters to the young in 1985, to families in 1994, to children in 1994, to women in 1995 and to artists in 1999 – not counting those letters that he wrote each year to priests on Holy Thursday, since the beginning of his pontificate – he wrote deeply moving and encouraging words to his peers in the Letter to the Elderly. He had no fear in placing before the eyes of the world the limits and frailties that the years had placed upon him. He did nothing to disguise them. John Paul II continued to fulfill his mission as the Successor of Peter, looking far ahead with the enthusiasm of the only youth that does not deteriorate, that of the spirit, which this pope maintained intact. The letter had a very personal, almost confidential tone, and was not an analysis of old age. Rather, it was a very intimate dialogue between people of the same generation.

"The passage of time," wrote the pope in that memorable letter, "helps us to see our experiences in a clearer light and softens their painful side." Moreover, he says, the daily difficulties can be eased with God's help. In addition, "we are consoled by the thought that, by virtue of our spiritual souls, we will survive beyond death."

"Guardians of shared memory" was the title of one part of the pope's Letter. Pointing out that "in the past, great respect was shown to the elderly," he remarks that this is still true in many cultures today, "while among others, this is much less the case, due to a mentality which gives priority to immediate human usefulness and productivity." He wrote: "It has come to the point where euthanasia is increasingly put forward as a solution for difficult situations. Unfortunately, in recent years the idea of euthanasia has lost for many people the sense of horror which it naturally awakens in those who have a sense of respect for life."

He added:

Here it should be kept in mind that the moral law allows the rejection of "aggressive medical treatment" and makes obligatory only those forms of treatment which fall within the normal requirements of medical care, which in the case of terminal illness seeks primarily to alleviate pain. But euthanasia, understood as directly causing death, is another thing entirely. Regardless of intentions and circumstances, euthanasia is always an intrinsically evil act, a violation of God's law and an offense against the dignity of the human person.

Pope John Paul II continued in that letter: "Man has been made for life, whereas death ... was not a part of God's original plan but came about as a consequence of sin. ... However rationally comprehensible death may be from a biological standpoint, it is not possible to experience it as something 'natural.'" We ask ourselves, he says here, "What is on the other side of the shadowy wall of death?" The answer comes from faith, "which illuminates the mystery of death and brings serenity to old age, now no longer lived passively as the expectation of a calamity, but rather as a promise-filled approach to the goal of full maturity."

The Letter to the Elderly closed with a section entitled "An encouragement to live life to the full." He writes:

> I feel a spontaneous desire to share fully with you my own feelings at this point of my life, after more than twenty years of ministry on the throne of Peter. ... Despite the limitations brought on by age I continue to enjoy life. For this I thank the Lord. It is wonderful to be able to give oneself to the very end for the sake of the Kingdom of God!

"At the same time," he concludes, "I find great peace in thinking about the time when the Lord will call me: from life to life! ... 'Bid me to come to you': this is the deepest yearning of the human heart, even in those who are not conscious of it." What a magnificent signature piece of Pope John Paul II! He not only wrote the letter but enacted it in his own life. We were eyewitnesses.

Suffering can be redemptive. The very worst pain and diminishment can set free the very best in people. Against the backdrop of a Culture of Death, where life is so cheap and sanctioned euthanasia is on our doorsteps, John Paul II's dying gave new meaning and urgency to the Gospel of Life in all of its agonizing beauty.

In a youth-obsessed culture in which people are constantly urged to fight or deny the ravages of time, age and disease, he reminded us that aging and suffering are a natural part of being human. Where the old and infirm are so easily put in nursing homes and often forgotten, the pope was a timely and powerful reminder that our parents and grandparents, the sick, the disabled and the dying have great value. Many young people have confided in me over the past few years that they were "deprived" of their grandparents in their families; they witnessed in the public diminishment and suffering of John Paul II the real meaning of aging and suffering. I have heard over and over again from young people these past years, "I feel as if he were my grandfather."

The public suffering

Pope John Paul II taught us that life is sacred, no matter how painful his own life became for him. We can only imagine his frustration and sadness in 2005 when he was unable to descend to St. Peter's Square to preside at the magnificent Palm Sunday liturgy (the 20th anniversary of World Youth Days) – where most of the 50,000-plus crowd was made up of young people. Instead, he sent those gathered a message: "I become more and more aware how providential and prophetic it is that this day, Palm Sunday and the Passion of the Lord, has become your day. This feast contains a special grace, that of joy united to the Cross which epitomizes the Christian mystery."

Many Catholics saw the pope's suffering as something like the agony of Jesus himself, and neither John Paul II nor those around him discouraged such comparisons. When asked if he might consider resigning, John Paul II reportedly asked, in reply, "Did Christ come down from the cross?" His close aides say that debate about his ability to administer the Church, as if he were the CEO of a secular corporation, essentially missed the point. This pope is not doing a job, he is carrying out a divine mission, and his pain is at its core.

9

"Dare to Be Saints!": John Paul II's Invitation to Holiness

Holiness is a truth that pervades the whole of the first covenant: God is holy and calls all to holiness. The Mosaic Law exhorted, "You shall be holy; for I the Lord your God am holy" (Leviticus 19:2). Holiness is in God, and only from God can it pass to the crown of God's creation: human beings. We are made in the image and likeness of God, and God's holiness, his "total otherness," is imprinted on each one of us. Human beings become vehicles and instruments of God's holiness for the world. This holiness is the fire of God's Word that must be alive and burning within our hearts. It is this fire, this dynamism, that will burn away the evil within us and around us and cause holiness to burst forth, healing and transforming the society and culture surrounding us. Evil is only eradicated by holiness, not by harshness. Holiness introduces into society a seed that heals and transforms.

Holiness is a way of life that involves commitment and activity. It is not a passive endeavour, but rather a continuous choice to deepen one's relationship with God and to then allow this relationship to guide all of one's actions in the world. Holiness requires a radical change in mindset and attitude. The acceptance of the call to holiness places God as our final goal in every aspect of our lives. This fundamental orientation toward God even envelops and sustains our relationship with other human beings. Sustained by a life of virtue and fortified by the gifts of the Holy Spirit, we are drawn by God ever closer to himself and to that day when we shall see him face to face in heaven and achieve full union with him. Here and now, we can find holiness in our personal experience of putting forth our best efforts in the workplace, patiently raising our children, and building good relationships at home, at school and at work. If we make all of these things a part of our loving response to God, we are on the path of holiness.

Jesus made his own the call to holiness that God spoke to the people of the first covenant. He repeated it continually by word and by the example of his life. Especially in the Sermon on the Mount, he left to the Church a code of Christian holiness. The history of Christian holiness is the proof that by living in the spirit of the Beatitudes proclaimed in the Sermon on the Mount (cf. Matthew 5:3-12), Christ's exhortation in the parable of the vine and the branches is realized: "Abide in me, and I in you ... He who abides in me, and I in him, bears much fruit" (John 15:4, 5). These words are verified in many ways in the lives of individual Christians, thereby showing, down through the centuries, the manifold riches and beauty of the holiness of the Church.

In his Apostolic Letter *Novo Millennio Ineunte*, at the close of the Great Jubilee of the Year 2000, John Paul II invited all "to place pastoral planning under the heading of holiness," to express

the conviction that, since Baptism is a true entry into the holiness of God through incorporation into Christ and the indwelling of his Spirit, it would be a contradiction to settle for a life of mediocrity, marked by a minimalist ethic and a shallow religiosity ... The time has come to re-propose wholeheartedly to everyone this high standard of ordinary Christian living: the whole life of the Christian community and of Christian families must lead in this direction. (n. 31)

The Church is the "home of holiness," and holiness is our most accurate image, our authentic calling card and our greatest gift to the world. It describes best who and what we are and strive to be.

John Paul II's invitation to holiness

Throughout his pontificate, and especially when he addressed young adults, John Paul II offered Jesus Christ as the One who "has become the friend of each one of us, the daily companion, contemporary and close to each person who lives, at whatever moment of human history."

The pope was convinced that young people are capable of holiness. He believed they were capable – not just "later," "in the future," but now. He believed that young people were capable of the heroic virtue on which true holiness is built. For that reason, he believed that young people could in fact set examples for us about the path to sanctity.

It's easy to point to the beatification of two of the young Fatima seers, Francisco and Jacinta, in Fatima in 2000. John Paul II said during his homily that this shows that even the very young – both died before they were teenagers – are capable of holiness. They were not martyrs, but saints, whose heroic virtues were established for all. They responded to Mary's call to pray, to do reparation and penance, and, even though it was hard, they did it.

John Paul II also cited the example of Saint Thérèse of the Child Jesus, whose "little way" was something that people of all ages, but especially the young, could follow. In declaring her a Doctor of the Church in 1997, despite the fact that she never went to high school, he declared that she was an "eminent teacher" of the faith. Thérèse understood that we are all called to be love in the heart of the Church, to be humble, to be little.

Blessed Pier Giorgio Frassati was another young holy person who lived a life of great charity, a life of the beatitudes, until his death in his mid 20s. In beatifying Frassati in St. Peter's Square on May 20, 1990, Pope John Paul II described Pier Giorgio as the "man of the eight Beatitudes," and said in his homily:

> By his example he proclaims that a life lived in Christ's Spirit, the Spirit of the Beatitudes, is "blessed", and that only the person who becomes a "man or woman of the Beatitudes" can succeed in communicating love and peace to others. He repeats that it is really worth giving up everything to serve the Lord. He testifies that holiness is possible for everyone, and that only the revolution of charity can enkindle the hope of a better future in the hearts of people. ... He left this world rather young, but he made a mark upon our entire century, and not only on our century.

The holy young mountain climber from Pollone shows us the way "verso l'alto", upward to heaven and deep into the heart of God. May all of us find in Blessed Pier Giorgio Frassati what Jesus' Sermon on a Galilean hillside really meant.

The pope spoke often of Francis of Assisi, and on April 21, 1981, said of this favourite son of Umbria:

> For him, the Gospel, and in particular the words of the Beatitudes, did not remain a fine text, or even an ideal,

but meant attitudes to be put into practice very concretely, almost literally. Because he was an unequalled witness to Christ, he brought forth in the Church a spiritual movement that many people no longer had dared to hope for.

Perhaps the greatest example of youthful holiness for John Paul II was Mary, who as a teenager said a full-hearted "yes" to the Lord's call and changed the history of the world. He dedicated his pontificate to her with the motto *Totus Tuus*.

John Paul II challenged young people to greatness. "Challenge" was one of his favourite terms. He called them to be "brave," to be "strong," to "have courage." He acknowledged their fears and often named them. He taught his dear young friends not to be afraid to be the morning watchmen for a new millennium. Not to be afraid to love purity. Not to be afraid to be saints. But he reminded them that courage is not the absence of fear, but the capacity to do what we should, despite our fears. John Paul II said that following Christ, putting out into the deep while trusting Christ, is the greatest adventure of all.

Saints of the new millennium

John Paul II spoke frequently to young people about the call to holiness and the vocation to be saints. Who can forget his message for World Youth Day 2000 in Rome? He wrote to his dear young friends throughout the world some unforgettable words that became the rallying cry for the Jubilee's greatest celebration:

Young people of every continent, do not be afraid to be the saints of the new millennium! Be contemplative, love prayer; be coherent with your faith and generous in the service of your brothers and sisters, be active members of the Church and builders of peace. To succeed in this demanding project of life, continue to listen to His Word, draw strength from the Sacraments, especially the Eucharist and Penance. The Lord wants you to be intrepid apostles of his gospel and builders of a new humanity.

Two years later, for World Youth Day 2002 in Canada, John Paul II took up once again the theme of holiness and saints in his message to the young people of the world:

Just as salt gives flavour to food and light illumines the darkness, so too holiness gives full meaning to life and makes it reflect God's glory. How many saints, especially young saints, can we count in the Church's history! In their love for God their heroic virtues shone before the world, and so they became models of life that the Church has held up for imitation by all. … Through the intercession of this great host of witnesses, may God make you too, dear young people, the saints of the third millennium!

At the concluding Mass of Canada's World Youth Day at Downsview Park on Sunday, July 28, 2002, Pope John Paul issued a stirring challenge that still resounds in North America, in particular, today:

And if, in the depths of your hearts, you feel the same call to the priesthood or consecrated life, do not be afraid to follow Christ on the royal road of the Cross! At difficult moments in the Church's life, the pursuit of holiness becomes even more urgent. And holiness is not a question of age; it is a matter of living in the Holy Spirit, just as Kateri Tekakwitha did here in [North] America and so many other young people have done.

John Paul II gave flesh and blood to the Beatitudes throughout his entire lifetime. He let us catch a glimpse of the greatness and holiness to which we are all called, and showed us the face of God as we journey on our pilgrim way on earth. A great part of the success of his message is due to the fact that he was surrounded by a tremendous cloud of witnesses who stood by him and strengthened him throughout his life. Is it any wonder, then, that millions of young people throughout the world loved him and took up his invitation to become "saints of the new millennium"?

The Church is the "home of holiness," and holiness is our most accurate image, our authentic calling card, and our greatest gift to the world. It describes best who and what we are and strive to be. In the life of Karol Wojtyla, holiness was contagious. Pope John Paul II was not only our Holy Father, but a Father who was and is holy. On April 2, 2005, he died a public death that stopped the world for several days. On April 8, 2005, Cardinal Joseph Ratzinger told the world that John Paul II was watching and blessing us "from the window of the Father's House."

Excerpt from the Homily of Benedict XVI at the Beatification of John Paul II

"Today our eyes behold, in the full spiritual light of the risen Christ, the beloved and revered figure of John Paul II. Today his name is added to the host of those whom he proclaimed

Prayer of St. Francis of Assisi

Lord, make me an instrument of
    Your peace.
Where there is hatred, let me sow
    love.
Where there is injury, pardon,
Where there is doubt, faith,
Where there is despair, hope,
Where there is darkness, light,
    and where there is sadness, joy.
O Divine Master, grant that I may
    not so much seek to be consoled,
    as to console;
To be understood, as to understand;
To be loved, as to love;
For it is in giving that we
    receive,
It is in pardoning that we are
    pardoned
And it is in dying that we are
    born to eternal life.

Feast Day: October 4

Patron of Catholic Action

saints and blesseds during the almost twenty-seven years of his pontificate, thereby forcefully emphasizing the universal vocation to the heights of the Christian life, to holiness, taught by the conciliar Constitution on the Church Lumen Gentium.

"All of us, as members of the people of God – bishops, priests, deacons, laity, men and women religious – are making our pilgrim way to the heavenly homeland where the Virgin Mary has preceded us, associated as she was in a unique and perfect way to the mystery of Christ and the Church.

"Karol Wojtyla took part in the Second Vatican Council, first as an auxiliary Bishop and then as Archbishop of Kraków. He was fully aware that the Council's decision to devote the last chapter of its Constitution on the Church to Mary meant that the Mother of the Redeemer is held up as an image and model of holiness for every Christian and for the entire Church. This was the theological vision that Blessed John Paul II discovered as a young man and subsequently maintained and deepened throughout his life. A vision that is expressed in the scriptural image of the crucified Christ with Mary, his Mother, at his side.

"… When Karol Wojtyla ascended to the throne of Peter, he brought with him a deep understanding of the difference between Marxism and Christianity, based on their respective visions of man. This was his message: man is the way of the Church, and Christ is the way of man. With this message, which is the great legacy of the Second Vatican Council and of its 'helmsman', the Servant of God Pope Paul VI, John Paul II led the People of God across the threshold of the Third Millennium, which thanks to Christ he was able to call 'the threshold of hope'.

Throughout the long journey of preparation for the great Jubilee he directed Christianity once again to the future, the future of God, which transcends history while nonetheless directly affecting it. He rightly reclaimed for Christianity that impulse of hope which had in some sense faltered before Marxism and the ideology of progress. He restored to Christianity its true face as a religion of hope, to be lived in history in an "Advent" spirit, in a personal and communitarian existence directed to Christ, the fullness of humanity and the fulfillment of all our longings for justice and peace. ...

"Blessed are you, beloved Pope John Paul II, because you believed! Continue, we implore you, to sustain from heaven the faith of God's people. You often blessed us in this Square from the Apostolic Palace: Bless us, Holy Father! Amen."

10

EMBRACING THE CROSS: JOHN PAUL II'S FINAL GOOD FRIDAY EVENING

One of my most vivid memories from the last week of John Paul II's life was during the Way of the Cross in Rome on Good Friday evening in 2005, in which he participated by watching the service at the Coliseum on television in his chapel. We were televising that moment from our broadcast centre in Toronto. The television camera in his chapel was behind him so he would not be distracted from taking part in this ceremony, in which he always took part personally. Then-Archbishop John Foley was doing the television commentary in English from Rome, reading the very provocative meditations prepared by a certain Joseph Cardinal Ratzinger.

At one point toward the end of the Way of the Cross, someone put a rather large crucifix on the knee of the Holy Father, and he was gazing lovingly at the figure of Jesus. At the words "Jesus dies on the cross," Pope John Paul drew the crucifix to himself and embraced it. I will never forget that scene. Those of us working in the master control room in Toronto had tears streaming down our faces. What an incredibly powerful homily without words! Like Jesus, Pope John Paul II embraced the cross; in fact, he embraced the crucifix of Jesus Christ on Good Friday night.

The death of a patriarch

During his final hours during the octave of Easter, a new generation wished to show they had understood his teaching, and so many of them gathered silently in prayer in St. Peter's Square and many other places around the world. Tens of thousands of young people were aware that his demise was a loss: "their" pope, whom they considered "their father in the faith," was dying. Though broken and bent at the end of his earthly pilgrimage, John Paul II crossed the threshold of history, standing as tall as a giant.

The pope of holiness

Karol Wojtyla himself was an extraordinary witness who, through his devotion, heroic efforts, long suffering and death, communicated the powerful message of the gospel to the men and women of our day. A great part of the success of his message is due to the fact that he was surrounded by a tremendous cloud of witnesses who stood by him and strengthened him throughout his life. For John Paul II, the call to holiness excludes no one; it is not the privilege of a spiritual elite.

Lumen Gentium, the Dogmatic Constitution on the Church of the Second Vatican Council, notes that the holiness of Christians flows from that of the Church and manifests it. It says that holiness "is expressed in many ways by the individuals who, each in his own state of life, tend to the perfection of love, thus sanctifying others" (n. 39). In this variety, "one and the same holiness is cultivated by all, who are moved by the Spirit of God ... and follow the poor Christ, the humble and crossbearing Christ in order to be worthy of being sharers in his glory" (n. 41).

John Paul II began his historic pontificate with the words that would become the refrain of the past 27 years: "Do not be afraid! Open wide the doors to Christ!" For many young Catholics throughout the world, those words did not fall on deaf ears. The very battle hymn that they made their own was "John Paul II, we love you!" He responded back to them: "John Paul II, he loves you." The young people of the generation of John Paul II are not to be dismissed. They are here to stay.

This has been proven time and again throughout the world, but especially so on the highways and byways of Canada. From St. John's, Newfoundland, to Vancouver, British Columbia, Canadians flocked to hear this holy giant. Like the hundreds of thousands of youth who gathered in Toronto in 2002, they, too, joined the chorus of "John Paul II, we love you!" The many schools and churches named after him since his death are only a modest testimony to the long reach of his personality and teaching in this country.

There is no doubt that John Paul II's successors will build on the foundation laid by the Polish pontiff, as well as completing much of the unfinished business that any human leader always leaves behind. We can only hope and pray that whoever the successors may be, they will keep the "John Paul II generation" at the heart of their Petrine ministry and service to the world. John Paul the actor gave the world a command performance on a world stage. To his "dear young friends," it was truly a master class in the drama of gospel living and dying.

In the words of William Shakespeare's *Romeo and Juliet*:

… when he shall die,
Take him and cut him out
    in little stars,
And he will make the face of heaven so fine
That all the world will be in love with night,
And pay no worship to the garish sun.

And in the words of Horatio, Hamlet's friend:

"Good night, sweet prince,
And flights of angels sing thee to thy rest!"

AFTERWORD

S ince the death of Pope John Paul II, I have had many opportunities to speak about him to various audiences and groups
around the world. Each occasion offered me an opportunity to
quietly give thanks to God for this great man's influence on my
life, and on the life of the Church and the world. But one occasion stands out in my mind, an unlikely, unique, unexpected
and grace-filled moment that allowed me to offer his memory
and legacy to the world. In early July 2007, I received an invitation, out of the blue, to lead a reflection for the AFL-CIO
International Convention of the Communications Workers of
America, being held at the Convention Centre in downtown
Toronto. Over 5,000 communications workers were present
from throughout North America. The organizers asked me
simply to speak for 30 minutes on any topic I chose that might
inspire the various labour unions' communications workers.
There was a rather awesome scene before me in the cavernous
hall on that summer morning. This is what I said:

Dear Friends,

Thank you for the invitation to be with you this morning at the 69th Convention of the Communications Workers of America, AFL-CIO. It is a privilege to stand before thousands of men and women working in the areas of communications, media, hospitality and travel from the United States of America and Canada – men and women who are truly ambassadors linking people together. In fact, we are all involved in the work of communications – of using words to build up, of connecting human beings across the face of the earth and giving deeper meaning to life.

I would like to speak to you about one of the greatest communicators who ever walked the face of the earth, and in particular this very earth of Toronto, only five years ago for World Youth Day 2002 – the Polish man born as Karol Wojtyla, whom you all knew as Pope John Paul II.

While Pope John Paul II did leave behind a spiritual testament that was read to the cardinals and later shared with the world after his death, his last major formal document was an Apostolic Letter entitled The Rapid Development, released on January 24, 2005. It was addressed "To Those Responsible for Communications" and contains an important message to every media mogul, copy editor, reporter, writer, broadcaster, web master, blogger and communications worker, whether Roman Catholic or not.

A "spirituality of communication" is one of the major contributions of the letter that is none other than John Paul's Testament on Social Communications. It is not a coincidence that the last document of this great Pope should be on the theme of Communications, for if any church leader ever embodied and exemplified the great communicator, it was John Paul II.

The contents of this remarkable document were somewhat eclipsed by the late pope's final suffering and death, and the election of his successor. In rapid development, John Paul II was concise in reviewing the Christian view of history: "Salvation History recounts and documents the communication of God with man, a communication which uses all forms and ways of communication." He then notes that history's greatest communicator, Jesus, used a variety of techniques:

> He explains the Scriptures, expresses himself in parables, dialogues within the intimacy of the home, speaks in the squares, along the streets, on the shores of the lake and on the mountaintops. The personal encounter with him does not leave one indifferent ….

John Paul II also stated that

> The media provides a providential opportunity to reach people everywhere, overcoming barriers of time, of space, and of language; presenting the content of faith in the most varied ways imaginable; and offering to all who search the possibility of entering into dialogue with the mystery of God, revealed fully in Christ Jesus.

John Paul II said that communicators, both within and outside the church, must apply in their own lives those values and behaviour that they are called to teach others. The communicator is not only one who practises his work, but someone who "lives" his work. As communicator, the person transmits a view and, therefore, becomes a witness. Communicators must be witnesses of values that are good for society. Communications and the media become instruments at the service of peace, at the service of the development of human society.

But there was also a warning and a challenge in this brief document: "Many people, in fact, believe that humanity must learn to live in a climate governed by an absence of meaning, by the provisional and by the fleeting."

Throughout his nearly 27-year pontificate, John Paul II taught us that communication is power. He told us to use that power wisely. Prudently get our message out and it will have a shot at bearing fruit, despite obstacles. And if anyone knew about obstacles, John Paul II did, having lived long and prospered, despite being faced from the very beginning with the tyranny of Nazism and then Communism.

As the curtain was about to fall for the last time for the Great Communicator John Paul II in early April 2005, the athlete was immobilized, the distinctive, booming voice silenced, and the hand that produced voluminous encyclicals no longer able to write. Yet nothing made him waver, even the debilitating sickness hidden under the glazed Parkinsonian mask, and ultimately his inability to speak and move. I am convinced that the most powerful message he preached was when the words and actions failed. It was then, in the passion of Karol Wojtyla, that the world saw what authentic communication was all about. Authentic communication is born of human solidarity and compassion.

The forces he partially unleashed against authoritarian regimes during his lifetime were only side-effects of the way the man who began life as Karol Wojtyla viewed humanity. At the beginning of the third millennium, we have economic globalization. But this must be accompanied by a moral globalization.

Whether or not one shares John Paul II's motivating beliefs, one can certainly acknowledge that his was the most impressive attempt so far made by any single human being to spell out what moral globalization might mean, starting with a lived practice of universal solidarity, charity and hope. And he did this by communicating his message boldly and respectfully wherever he went.

He taught us that there is much more to the Church and the papacy than preaching, speaking, writing, greeting people and travelling – although he certainly did enough of all of that. He communicated through spontaneous, symbolic actions that were often more eloquent than some of his speeches, homilies and encyclicals – especially his final moments on the world stage. Those actions were often powerful symbols.

The word "symbol" comes from the Greek word *symbolein* – "to bring together"; it's the opposite of the Greek word *diabolein*, "to break apart, to divide" – the origin of our word "diabolical." Symbolic actions help to bring people together in peace and in love. Up to the moment of his death – and even after, Pope John Paul II was bringing people together in peace and in love. This is communication at the service of truth. Who can ever forget his global funeral that brought the world to a standstill in April 2005?

We had in John Paul a brilliant teacher, communicator and model of goodness and humanity; a wise communicator who would become a "Pontifex Massmediaticus". He began his historic service to the world with words that would become the refrain of the past 27 years: "Do not be afraid!" Would that many of us in the Church, in the media world, in our unions and professions, take these words to heart! Think of the walls that might come tumbling down! Imagine the bridges that would be built!

And so I pray for you and with you today these words in light of the life and example of a great communicator, Karol Wojtyla, now the Servant of God, Pope John Paul II:

May you be praised, Lord,
for the communicators and communications workers,
writers, artists, directors,
and all those whose gifts light up
both theatre and cinema and provide audiences
with heightened awareness of their human condition.

May you be praised, Lord,
for all those who labour painstakingly with words
especially in our newspapers, journals and magazines –
those who try to communicate with us the mystery,
the truth and the beauty of human life.

Help all of the communications workers and media
experts
gathered here today in Toronto to be deeply convinced
of the great vocation
you give to each person to build bridges, not walls,
to make their words become flesh so that the blind may
see, the deaf hear,

and the poor may have the Good News proclaimed
to them by all who rejoice in their God-given talents
and their gift of splendid creativity.

May the Servant of God John Paul II touch each of you
and help you not to be afraid of serving the truth and
loving life.

Amen.

I have prayed to him every single day, asking this holy man
of God and great communicator to watch over us in Canada,
and most especially to guide Salt and Light Catholic Media
Foundation and Television Network. I have no doubt in my
mind that if we are alive today, and if we can serve the Church
in the area of communications, it is because Saint John Paul II
stands at the window of the Father's house, watching over us
and blessing us.

O Blessed Trinity,

We thank you for having graced the Church with
    Pope John Paul II
and for allowing the tenderness of your Fatherly care,
the glory of the cross of Christ,
and the splendour of the Holy Spirit to shine through him.

Trusting fully in Your infinite mercy
and in the maternal intercession of Mary,
he has given us a living image of Jesus the Good Shepherd,
and has shown us that holiness
is the necessary measure of ordinary Christian life
and is the way of achieving eternal communion with you.

Grant us, by his intercession, and according to Your will,
the graces we implore,
knowing that he is now numbered among your saints.
Amen.